Awesome Mother-Daughter Relationship

How to build and maintain a life-time beautiful bond between mother and daughter

BY

SARAH CHAPMAN

TABLE OF CONTENT

Introduction

CHAPTER TWO

How to improve your mother-daughter relationship

- Let her talk, love to listen…

- Learn what she loves and learn to love it too…

- Don't react to any "drama"

- Teach her what you know…

- Talk to her about her relationships…

CHAPTER THREE

How to grow mother-daughter relationship

- Try to find time in your schedule to do things with your daughter.

- Knowing what kinds of activities your daughter enjoys will help greatly when you spend time together because you'll know what to do and where to go.

- If there's one thing that will build girls' relationships, it's shopping. You'll have a chance to talk and find more about your daughter's interests while getting new things

- If you don't want to shop, there are still plenty of options

- As a mom, it's important that you should support your daughter in her education.

- Another way to interact with your daughter is through playing a great game

- Another fun way for the two of you to bond is through cooking or baking

- Of course, your daughter already knows that you love her, but do you really show it?

- It's important for your daughter to know that she can always come and talk to you if she needs anything.

- Listen

- Try to be around for your daughter.

- Be encouraging.

- Celebrate your daughter's talents.

- Be kind to her.

- Trust your daughter as best you can.

CHAPTER FOUR

How to Be Your Daughter's Best Friend

- Spend tons of time together – working and playing.

- You're her dear friend, but not her buddy.

- Bring Dad in when you can't work it out

- Don't be overprotective

- Respect her choices

- Be there for her

- Spend time with her

- Give your daughter her alone' time

- Respect her choices

SUMMARY

Introduction

The relationship between a mother and daughter is special. A mother's love for her daughter cannot be described in words. Some things are hard to say, but it can be felt. The bond between a mother and daughter is strong, and the mother-daughter bonding can start at an early age. However, sometimes, the relationship between a mother and her daughter may get a little complicated.

Building a friendship with your daughter is one of the most lovely rewards a mother can enjoy. You only have to walk into the room and she intuitively understands what's behind your smile. Or quietly gives you that little hug when you're down

While some might think strictness and discipline will help them raise their kids better, there are many who think being their kid's friend should be given utmost importance. No matter which category of parents you belong to, you can do both things at the same time- being your child's best friend and raising them well.

On some days, you might go shopping with your daughter and have fun or just sit with her at home and listen to her when she tells you about her big dreams and future plans, but there will also be days when your daughter would not listen to you or disobey you. At that time, you might feel that your relationship is falling apart, but deep down you'd know that your daughter loves you. Yes, in her teenage years she might behave a little strange, but she will come around. And it is during these years that you will have to work hard on your relationship.

CHAPTER ONE

Why is a Mother-Daughter Relationship Important?

The relationship that a girl shares with her mother can affect her sense of self-esteem, self-worth, sense of identity, and her ability to make friends. Children who are encouraged and praised (healthy praise, of course!) by their parents grow up to be confident individuals. If a child is not appreciated by her parents, she may seek validation from others.

When a girl is in her teenage years, she usually looks up to her mother. Her mother is her role model and she wishes to be like her. She gets her perfect image of a woman from her mother. But the relationship between a mother and daughter can go through many ups and downs. Many things can derail the harmonious relationship between a mother and her daughter. Temperaments, personality, experiences, hormones can all affect their relationship. Whatever may be the cause, it can be worked upon.

How to Build and Maintain a Strong Bond with Your Daughter

Here are some ways to help you improve your bond with your daughter:

1. *When She is a Little Girl*

It is important to forge a strong connection from the very start, i.e., soon after the birth of your daughter. Some things to keep in mind are as follows:

Breastfeed Your Daughter

By breastfeeding your little angel, you can develop a strong bond with her. The release of oxytocin hormone (the love hormone) during breastfeeding makes the mother fall in love with her baby even more, and this only helps in improving the bond between mother and daughter. Breastfeed your daughter in the first six months of her life. You can also enlist the help of a trained nurse to assist you with the task. Also, hold and cuddle your baby as much as possible to make her feel loved, comfortable, and safe. If you are unable to breastfeed your baby for some reason, try to maintain skin contact with her. Skin-to-skin contact between the mother and her child also strengthens the bond between the two.

Set a Routine

Spend some time with your daughter daily. Plan special weekend trips or getaways with your daughter. This will strengthen your bond.

A mother and her daughter play dress up

You can play dress up with your daughter, comb her hair, or brush her teeth while she is young – all these activities will bring you two closer. In case your daughter tries to imitate you, let her. Take it as an opportunity to model good behavior. Also, encourage her to love her imperfections and try to find good in the negative things.

1.Express Your Affection Openly

Express your affection to her openly. If your daughter does something good, let her know that you are proud of her. This shows how much you love her. Nurture your bond with your daughter by sharing hugs, cuddles, and kisses. For example, you can incorporate extensive cuddle time during bedtime. These physical acts of love may teach your daughter to freely demonstrate and accept affection.

The greatest gift you can give your daughter while she is young is your time. Take out time from your schedule to focus and spend some time with her to let her know that you value her as an individual. Make her feel special by sharing your joys and sorrows with her. Also, involve her in household chores from an early age to develop a sense of responsibility in her.

2. When She is a Teenager/Adult

When a girl is in her teenage years, it can be a difficult time for her. A daughter needs her mother the most in her teenage years and also when she gets married. Here is what you will need to remember when your daughter becomes a teenager:

3. **Be Her Guide**

Adolescence can be a difficult phase for your girl because, at that time, she will try to find her identity and will struggle to cope up with the various physical and emotional changes she will go through. Make sure you provide her necessary guidance and support, and hear her out. Do offer her advice, but don't command her as she might become rebellious. Just listen to her concerns and try to channelise her stress or anger positively.

4. **Respect Her Feelings**

Honor your daughter's boundaries. As much as you may prefer to be with her, if she desires some 'alone time', give that to her. On some days, you might make mistakes too. Be a bigger person and own up to your mistakes. Simply apologize and make amends. Respect her individuality and allow her to explore her inner worth and interests without inhibition.

Talk to Her Freely

Talk to your daughter about various worldly issues. You can share your pearls of wisdom while going shopping with her or while cooking meals. As a teenager, she may feel insecure about her body. Help her accept and be proud of her body. Talk to her about relationships, character traits like faith, integrity, perseverance, and courage. Let her know that these are the values she will need the most in her life. Empower and equip her with all your wisdom and life experiences.

OnKeep Realistic Expectations

As parents, it is normal to have certain expectations from children. But it is important to be reasonable. Remember your daughter is a separate individual who may have her dreams and aspirations. Give her space to grow and blossom by giving ample support and love.

It is a mother who educates her daughters about different things. It is a mother who teaches her daughter how to handle and carry herself in this world and how to deal with different sets of people and sail through various walks of life. A mother is the first friend of her daughter, who guides her throughout lives. If you have a daughter, make sure you are always there for her and support her in all walks of life.

CHAPTER TWO

How to improve your mother-daughter relationship

As moms, we have the opportunity to teach our girls how to grow up in this world—to be their guide, confidant, and friend for life. To do that we must maintain a connection even in difficult seasons of our relationship. So, how do you build that bond if you don't have a natural connection? Or, how can you strengthen it if you've already got a bond? There are a few things that I always tried to do—especially while my girls still lived at home—that helped me bond with them.

1. Let her talk, love to listen…
We've all heard the statistics about how many more words women speak per day than men. Our girls are women in the making so we should not be surprised when they talk—a lot. Women are natural

verbal communicators. Carve out time to spend with your daughter when there aren't distractions and you can really listen. Bedtime is a great moment for this with younger girls because they really don't want to go to bed and will happily chat. With your older girls, I learned to follow them to their room every time they walked in the door from school, from swim practice or from a night out—no matter how late it was. I would busy myself hanging up clothes for them as they decompressed after a long day. Lots of information would tumble out. Ask some open-ended questions, and then listen. Resist the urge to rush in to give advice. Just enjoy hearing her heart about whatever is bubbling to the top.

2. Learn what she loves and learn to love it too…

What makes your daughter tick? Is it dance? A sport? Music? Perhaps she's really into fashion. Whatever her passion is, invest in it with her. My girls love the theater. Over the years it has become our thing to do together. For every big birthday, if I ask what they want they say "Let's go to New York and see _____ on Broadway." We now have favorite restaurants, shops, and sights. NY has become one of several traditions with my girls that I treasure because we don't live together anymore.

3. **Don't react to any "drama"**

As I mentioned in the first point, we shouldn't be surprised at the statistics that women generally talk more than men do. And much to the first point, as you are listening to her spill her heart out to you, control your reactions to whatever she says. She is bound to say something that is dramatic or inflated, and your motherly instincts will kick in to correct or protect her. But that response has the potential of shutting her down from opening up again—she might be scared to say something wrong or offensive. Ask questions instead.

4. *Teach her what you know...*

Your life might look exactly like what your daughter wants to grow up to be, or perhaps it is far from it. It isn't the washing the dishes or folding the laundry that she needs you to teach her (although, those are helpful things for her to know while she's still at home!), but she needs you to teach her things that speak to her character. Things such as perseverance, faith, and integrity are essential traits that she will need to enter into the world. Equip her with as much as you know, and she will desire your opinion when she's out of the house. When my girls ask me for advice it makes me so happy to still be a part of their life.

5. ***Talk to her about her relationships...***
Why is it that girls have such a difficult time with friendships growing up? It's no secret that girls can be catty, jealous, and downright competitive with one another—and for no good reason. She needs you to show her what a good female to female relationship looks like. How do you communicate with your friends? Does your daughter feel comfortable around her friends? Or is she altering her personality to fit what she thinks they want her to be? But most importantly, model a healthy marriage relationship with your husband to show her

what a real life marriage looks like. She will be watching for one day when she finds herself in the same position!

Face it. You don't always bond with your daughter. She might be busy on the computer, the phone, with her friends, or with schoolwork. When you try to talk to her, she doesn't listen, or just leaves the room. She thinks that you are embarrassing, and you don't know how to change that.

You may be busy as well, with work, family, money, and so much more. Do either of these situations sound like you? If so, you need to improve your mother-daughter relationship and overall bond.

It might sound hard, but after a while, you'll realize that it isn't as hard as you thought. After all, she is your daughter. If, though, you still don't know how to have fun with her and find a common bond, don't worry. Just read this article for all the help you'll need.

CHAPTER THREE

How to grow mother-daughter relationship

Trust can be difficult, but it's the key basis of any relationship. If you find yourself doing untrustworthy things frequently, stop. If you lie often and catch her lying a lot, for instance, start being honest yourself. Always keep your promises; if something comes up that prevents you from keeping a promise, be sure to let her know about it.

If your daughter broke your trust, it may not be your fault. Let her know calmly and gently that you're unhappy with her and why she broke your trust. Then tell her what you'd like her to do better in the future.

When you see your daughter do something responsible, like chores, homework or band practicing, you can trust her more. Pat her on the back when she succeeds and gets good grades.

Share your feelings. Tell your daughter that she can always come to you if she needs to, and that she should be honest. You should share your feelings with her as well. Tell your daughter how you really feel about something, and sometimes, you can ask her for advice.

Try to find time in your schedule to do things with your daughter. Pick a certain day of the week or time of the day when both you and she are free, like Sundays or Thursday nights. It's good to do it the same day and time so you and she can remember when your special time together is, and you will be more likely to be free. Summer is a great time to do things together because your daughter will likely be out of school. If you are still working in summer, try to find time on the weekends to spend with your daughter. Ask for fewer hours at work, if you have to. Aim for at least an hour or two a day to spend with your daughter. Pick a time when your daughter is free, as well as you. Ask her, "Do you want to do something on _________ night?" Or, ask her when she is free, you'll be sure to find sometime. However, on weeknights, your child will probably be quite busy with her schoolwork. Respect that, and find a different time to spend together.

Knowing what kinds of activities your daughter enjoys will help greatly when you spend time together because you'll know what to do and where to go. Observe your child sometimes, but not too often, to see what they are doing. They might be on the computer, TV, drawing, reading, or playing outside. Look more into what she is doing, though, to get more clues into what she likes. If she is reading, ask her what she is reading. If she is watching TV, ask her what she is watching, and if she is on the computer or outside, ask her what she is playing. You'll get a better feel for what she likes, and when you ask, she'll feel glad that you are interested in what she is doing. Her interests may be very different from yours, but don't try to change what she likes and dislikes.[1]
Try to learn more about your daughter's interests yourself, and do things relating to

those activities. If she likes reading, for example, read together at home or spend an afternoon at the library. If she likes soccer, play a game or two in your backyard or the park. If your daughter likes painting or drawing, take her to an art museum.

If there's one thing that will build girls' relationships, it's shopping. You'll have a chance to talk and find more about your daughter's interests while getting new things. Take her with you to the grocery store to help you pick out dinner or delicious snacks. Have her put some items in the cart that she likes, and help decide what drinks to buy. If your daughter loves to read, go to a local bookstore and look for some books together. Or, go to a shopping mall. Look for clothes and shoes. You could also have her help you pick out clothes for yourself. She'll love to be your "fashion consultant", especially if she's into fashion. You can also go to a toy store if your daughter is younger.

Let her go by her style. When shopping for clothes, shoes, books, or anything, especially with teens, let your daughter pick what she likes. She's just expressing herself and being herself, she is her own person. You could always ask, "Do you like this?", but don't force her to buy and wear something she doesn't really like. Shop at a store your daughter really enjoys so she'll be more likely to find something she likes.

If you don't want to shop, there are still plenty of options*. Some are the pool,* park, beach, restaurant, museum, or amusement park. Now that you know your daughter's interests, you can start to know where she might want to go. Like stated before, pick somewhere that she would like. Take your baseball lover to her favorite team's game, or an artist to the arts and crafts store. Another important factor is the weather. Check online, on TV, or in the newspaper for details on the weather. Save outdoor activities like theme parks and the pool for sunny days. If it's winter, go to a cafe for some hot chocolate or make a snowman. You can always go in your backyard and play with your daughter, no matter the weather. Make a snow fort, have a snowball fight, make snow angels, or make a snowman. If your daughter likes sports, go skiing, sledding, or snowboarding. And don't fret if it's raining. Go to a movie theater, a restaurant, an indoor pool, the library, museum, really anywhere indoors.[2]

As a mom, it's important that you should support your daughter in her education. Always try to help her with homework if she asks for it. Don't give her the answer, help her. For example, if she is struggling with a math problem, don't just say "32". Say, "You have to ________" while still having her interact. Go through the steps with her, for example, "Then you multiply. What is 9 times 13?" so she'll know what to do next time. Also try to help her if she doesn't ask for it, but you get a hint that she needs help. If she's been doing homework for a long time, ask her if she needs any help

she can always come to you. Same with if your daughter got a poor grade on a test.[3] Make learning fun. Turn studying for a spelling or vocab test into a game of Jeopardy. Or, have your daughter be the teacher, teaching you about it.
Study with her. There might be an important test coming up, so it's your job to help her study. She'll probably tell you what to do e.g. Give me the word and I'll say the definition.

Another way to interact with your daughter is through playing a great game. Have a game night with the two of you on a certain day, or just ask her if she'd like to play a game. Some good family games you might want to play are Sorry, Monopoly, Life, Scrabble, Taboo, and Snakes and Ladders, but you could really play any game. Card games are also fun. Play Bluff, War, Go Fish, or UNO if you have a spare deck.

Another fun way for the two of you to bond is through cooking or baking. It's also a good way to start teaching them how to cook if they are older. Bring out some cookbooks and look through them with your daughter to see what to make. You can make cookies, a cake, cupcakes, cookies, brownies, or any dessert. You could also make your own bread or bagels, make a tart, crisp, smoothies, soup, stew, or even your own ice cream!

Remember that you are cooking together. Let your daughter do some things, like cracking eggs, helping whisk the batter, pouring liquids, and decorating. Expect things to not be done perfectly – this is how children and teens learn. However, do not let her use the oven until you believe she is mature and responsible enough to deal with working around heat on her own (by the same token, don't mollycoddle her forever – children should be able to deal with cooking with heat around the age of 11 or 12).

Of course, your daughter already knows that you love her, but do you really show it? Although playing a game or watching TV is spending time together, is it really quality special time? You may not know how to do this, but it's the little things that count. Go for a nice walk together, talk, and enjoy nature. Cheer her up on a bad day with a hug or a small gift, like a book or a stuffed animal. Give encouraging messages often, like "You can do it", "I believe in you", or "You are a very talented artist/swimmer/soccer player!". Be sure to praise her efforts above all, as it is important to let her know that it is in the trying and the doing, including learning to deal with failure, that she is going to succeed in life. With support from you, she'll be left with a positive attitude. Laugh and smile with her.[4]

It's important for your daughter to know that she can always come and talk to you if she needs anything. When you talk to your daughter, make sure that you look at her, and she does the same. Tell her, "I need you to listen" but in a calm, friendly way. Try to stay short and sweet, or your daughter will get bored, not focus, and think that they are in trouble or being lectured.

Leave the key point for the first sentence, and keep it simple, using non-confusing and/or shorter words. You should also occasionally talk casually. When the two of you talk, it shouldn't all be serious. Talk about school e.g. What's going on in school? How was school today? But, you should also go deeper than that. Ask her about her future, sports, or hobbies.[5]

It's important for your daughter to know that she can always come and talk to you if she needs anything. When you talk to your daughter, make sure that you look at her, and she does the same. Tell her, "I need you to listen" but in a calm, friendly way. Try to stay short and sweet, or your daughter will get bored, not focus, and think that they are in trouble or being lectured. Leave the key point for the first sentence, and keep it simple, using non-confusing and/or shorter words. You should also occasionally talk casually. When the two of you talk, it shouldn't all be serious. Talk about school e.g. What's going on in school? How was school today? But, you should also go deeper than that. Ask her about her future, sports, or hobbies.[5]

Listen.
Not only should your daughter listen to you, but you must listen as well. If you don't, she'll think it's okay to not pay attention— also be aware that children know when their parents aren't truly listening and it isn't a pleasant feeling because it is dis-empowering. To listen, stop what you are doing to look at her. Have good eye contact with each other so you can listen. To show that you are listening, ask her questions that you have. Also, paraphrase. Paraphrasing is putting something in your own words. Say, for example, "So you're saying _______" or "You mean that _______?" so you can clarify what your daughter just said to you.[6]
Listen to what she wants to do. For example, if your daughter wants to go to a movie, don't just say "No" right away. See what you can do; look at what movies are playing, or ask her what movie she wants to see. You might not want to do it, but

once in a while you should let your daughter get her way.

Try to be around for your daughter.
You need to always be there, whether it's through presence at an important event, advice, or by words of encouragement. If there is a sports, musical, school, or any important event that your daughter wants you to attend, really try to see if you can go. If not, see why. Try to cancel whatever it is that's on the same day, but some things you absolutely cannot miss, so be sure to tell your daughter. But it's okay if you can't actually be present at an event. There are lots of more ways to be there for your daughter.
Offer help. If you see your daughter struggling in anything, like school, sports, or an instrument, help her. Listen to her play her flute, contact the teacher or help with her schoolwork, or play basketball with her.

Be encouraging.
It may be hard for her to do something, so you must cheer her on and use

encouraging words and actions. Say "good job" when you truly mean it, and maybe get her a gift that says "way to go!", such as a book.

Compliment her. Say, for instance, "That's a nice shirt" or "I like what you did to your room".

Celebrate your daughter's talents.

This is another form of encouragement, and it will make your daughter feel so happy inside when you recognize her talents. Ask her if she would like to try out for a school play, strings solo, or softball team inside or outside of school (but don't be forceful), and she might agree. See if you can get her into a class or team, too. Another thing to do is to participate in the activity she's trying out elsewhere. Play a game or soccer, hold a concert at home, or have her teach you some dance moves. It will make her feel great, you'll learn something new, and the two of you will bond more.

Be kind to her.

This may go without saying, but your kindness has a huge impact on your relationship together. Don't yell at her right away when things don't go accordingly. Instead, remain calm and nice when explaining that she has done something you don't like or don't want her to do again. Try saying, "I want you to do this" or "please do this" instead of "do this" or "do this now". She's more likely to do what you say, anyway, if you address her kindly. Moreover, give real reasons, not just "because I said so." She will be more responsive if she realizes there are dangers, social pressure or poor health outcomes etc. likely to occur as a result of certain choices she makes. Also, hug and kiss her before she goes to bed, or in the morning before she leaves– always end everything on a good note.

Respect her. She is an individual, and you must remember that. There may be some things about your daughter that you may not quite agree with or understand, but still be respectful; she can have her own opinion.

Trust your daughter as best you can.

Trust can be difficult, but it's the key basis of any relationship. If you find yourself doing untrustworthy things frequently, stop. If you lie often and catch her lying a lot, for instance, start being honest yourself. Always keep your promises; if something comes up that prevents you from keeping a promise, be sure to let her know about it.

If your daughter broke your trust, it may not be your fault. Let her know calmly and gently that you're unhappy with her and why she broke your trust. Then tell her what you'd like her to do better in the future.

When you see your daughter do something responsible, like chores, homework or band practicing, you can trust her more. Pat her on the back when she succeeds and gets good grades.

Share your feelings. Tell your daughter that she can always come to you if she needs to, and that she should be honest. You should share your feelings with her as well. Tell your daughter how you really feel about something, and sometimes, you can ask her for advice….

CHAPTER FOUR

How to Be Your Daughter's Best Friend

Don't expect her to be just like you. As mothers, we can be rather taken aback when a girl, our very own girl birthed out of our very own bodies, can be so different from ourselves. And it can bother us. Or even hurt our feelings. We somehow want her to be created in our image, rather than in her Creator's image.

I believe this expectation is often the biggest barrier to a relationship between a mother and daughter. So if your daughter turns out to be surprisingly unlike you, that's okay! Rejoice in the gift that she is and seek for common interests . . . and even stretch yourself to enjoy her interests which might be different from your own.
As my girls started getting older, I began to communicate that I'm not only a mommy – I'm a real person with thoughts, feelings, and interests of my own.
This can be a strange concept to a child who initially (and rightfully) considers you

only as someone who is there to love and meet her needs. Yet as she matures, I want her to start thinking of me as a woman too. I might do this by sharing an excerpt from a book I'm enjoying, or talk about a project which I find exciting, or mention something that's made me happy or sad.

A mother-daughter bond is one of the special ones in the world. While some might think strictness and discipline will help them raise their daughters better, there are many who think being their daughter's friend should be given utmost importance. No matter which category of parents you belong to, you can do both things at the same time- being your child's best friend and raising them well. Here are a few ways you can befriend them:

Spend tons of time together – working and playing.

Don't merely love your daughter by serving her. Love her enough to pull her into your world and work together to get things done. It's strangely bonding when women accomplish something together, don't you think? I love grabbing a girl or two and diving into a kitchen project or a cleaning job. Before we know it, we're laughing and talking and having a wonderful time.

But we enjoy having special times together too. When the girls were young we had a weekly evening where we all worked on a craft. Now that the girls are older, we have tea-time nearly every day. It's usually a pleasant time to catch-up with each other, but occasionally a chance to talk through an issue. This is Girl Time.

You're her dear friend, but not her buddy.

I treasure the friendship of my girls. But that doesn't make us "buddies". In other words, I don't appreciate being spoken to or treated in a manner that suggests I'm one of her peers. Friendship notwithstanding, she needs to show me the respect due me as her mother. Sometimes she might start to get a bit cheeky or a little too palsy-walsy and I'll remind her that she still gets to honor me, even if we are friends.

Bring Dad in when you can't work it out.

So if I'm a woman. And she's a woman. And we both have emotions running strong – what then?

More than once, I've asked my husband to step in and help us out. It might be because I've lost perspective or have been so offended that I can't seem to "rise above" it. At that point, I'm particularly grateful for his steady nature and clear mind to set her (or me!) straight again. His involvement has been invaluable during those times when feminine passions are soaring at an all-time high.

Don't be overprotective

Though it is essential to ensure your daughters are going in the right direction and are safe, being overprotective is what ruins the relationship. Teach her about what is wrong and what is right, but let her decide for herself. Give her enough space to choose what she wants. In this way, she will not only trust you but will also be confident of her decisions.

Respect her choices

Be it choosing clothes to choosing profession, some mothers/parents just never let their daughters make the choice for themselves. This habit can turn toxic with time and can lower your daughter"s confidence too. Make sure you let your daughter make her life choices. You can surely advise her along the way, but dictating her life is something you should avoid.

Be there for her

Sometimes all that your daughter needs is someone to be there for her. She might be having troubles at school or might be going through something she wants to discuss with you. Give her the window of trust and instill her confidence that she can come and talk to you. In such a way, slowly and gradually your child will start sharing more and more things with you.

Spend time with her

Try to take out time from your busy schedule to spend time with her. Often girls complain that their mothers don't give them enough time, which makes them feel ignored and dejected. You can watch their favorite movie together, take them out to their favorite place or even cook something together. This will help you and your girls bond more.

Respect her choices

Be it choosing clothes to choosing profession, some mothers/parents just never let their kids make the choice for themselves. This habit can turn toxic with time and can lower your daughter's confidence too. Make sure you let your child make her life choices. You can surely advise her along the way, but dictating her life is something you should avoid.

Give your daughter her alone' time

Sometimes it is best to leave your daughter alone. No matter what your child's age is, everyone goes through a phase in which they want some alone time. Don't panic if your daughter starts spending more time

alone. It is probably just a phase, which will go away with time. Give her a comforting window, to which she can come anytime and share anything she wants to.
This will for sure improve your bond with your daughter and help you in becoming your child's best friend for life.

SUMMARY

The relationship between a woman and her mother is so powerful, it affects everything from her health and self-esteem to all her other relationships, experts say. Dr Christiane Northrup, author of the book Mother-Daughter Wisdom (Hay House), says: "The mother-daughter relationship is the most powerful bond in the world, for better or for worse. It sets the stage for all other relationships."
Jennie Hannan, executive general manager of services at counseling provider Anglicare WA, agrees. "How a woman sees herself, how she is in her adult relationships with partners, and how she mothers her own children, is profoundly influenced by her relationship with her own mother," she says. But while most five-year-old girls love their mothers with an unshakeable conviction, it's often a different story by the time they reach adolescence. The once-adored woman who rarely puts a foot wrong is suddenly always doing embarrassing things.

Different phases

"The time you are going to start having major problems with your daughter will be around adolescence," Hannan says. "Adolescence is a very difficult, tumultuous time for children and their parents, and it tends to happen in girls earlier than in boys."

Fortunately this wild swing from closeness to remoteness usually only lasts until the daughter reaches adulthood. "If the mother and daughter can hang in there during adolescence, your relationship moves to a different level and becomes more of a respectful friendship," Hannan says.

"I think what triggers them coming back is they become independent ... They move away from home, get a job, and do adult things in life. There's a need to grow up and the relationship shifts."

The relationship will change again when the daughter has children. "There's a greater level of understanding of the sort of depth of responsibility that you have as a mother to that child." If you had a less-than-perfect relationship with your mother, it doesn't necessarily follow that you won't have a good relationship with your own daughter.

"It gives you a head start if you had a good relationship with your mother, but lots of women who have had bad relationships with their mothers have had really positive relationships with other women in their lives.

"The idea that you can have a perfect relationship with anybody is flawed. Mothers do get blamed an awful lot if something's wrong with their kids. But being aware of things that were good and not good in your relationship with your mum is really important in not repeating any mistakes."

For most, the mother-daughter relationship is ultimately fulfilling. Despite conflicts and complicated emotions, 80 to 90 per cent of women at midlife reported a good relationship with their mother, a Pennsylvania State University study found.

"The relationship between mothers and their adult daughters is one in which the participants handle being upset with one another better than in any other relationship,"There is value in the mother-daughter tie because the two parties care for one another and share a strong investment in the family as a whole."

Forging a strong bond with your own daughter
"I'm a big believer in mother-daughter time," Anglicare WA's Jennie Hannan says. "I think we underestimate how important it is for mums and daughters to do things together in those early years. Doing that builds a foundation that will help you get through adolescence." Here are some ideas:

Go on regular special outings just the two of you. "Even just going to the park, when your daughter is little, will be worthwhile," Hannan says. Start mother-daughter traditions, such as going on long walks together, dining at a favorite restaurant or spending time together updating family photo albums. Go shopping together. Make something together - cookies, a cake, an egg-carton caterpillar. Watch a movie together, even if it's just at home on the couch.

Keeping things on an even keel with your mum is not always easy, as many celebrity mother-daughter relationships demonstrate.

It's never too late to repair your relationship Try a counseling session on your own first to help you work out whether or not it will be helpful to attend counseling with your mother or daughter.
Sometimes it's not possible to repair things that happened long ago. Instead, focus on working out how you would like to treat each other now.
Even if your mother has passed away, if you have unresolved issues you could benefit from counseling sessions. "Sometimes talking through the possibilities

of why something might have occurred can help you get some perspective.

There is truly nothing like a beautiful and healthy mother-daughter relationship. Mothers have such power to help mold their daughters into kind, confident, and grateful human beings. Likewise, daughters can enrich their mother's lives and add so much beauty to their existence.

It's safe to say that mother-daughter relationships aren't always easy, but we all have the power to build healthy connections that make life so much more fulfilling and beautiful.

As you navigate through your days as a mother and/or daughter, I hope you'll revel in your bond. We each have one life to live, and I am so thankful each day that I get to strengthen the bond with both my mother and my daughter.

If you've been at odds with your mother or your daughter, thankfully you have today to reconnect and start forging a stronger connection. I think the secret is in your

willingness to be vulnerable, real, raw, and forgiving. No K
For my friends who have lost your moms or daughters, I weep for you. May the love you forged burn bright inside.